AF477963

"Universally Despised"

Is My Skin The Sin?

Dedication

This book is dedicated to African and Black people all over the World past and present. It is also dedicated to those who have fought against the four riders of the Apocalypse, **IMPERIALISM, WAR, FAMINE, AND DEATH.** Further It is dedicated to those who have fought against **SLAVERY, COLONIALISM, and COLOR RACISM which is WHITE SUPREMACY** at its worse.

Special Dedication

It is an honor to offer this distinctive dedication to my son, Azariah Gabriel Brown Sr. I am so proud of him and his accomplishments, one of which is his being the first to establish a Mobile Barber shop in Austin, Texas. This achievement is being recognized by the Library of Congress.

I could not be any prouder!

Dad

Preface

This book is about Black people and what white supremacy has done to them. There is a term frequently used called "people of color". My response to that is, Do I look like a rainbow? Thus, the title UNIVERSALLY DESPISED, IS MY SKIN THE SIN and it deals with PEOPLE OF AFRICAN DESCENT AND BLACK PEOPLE ALL THROUGH THE AFRICAN DIASPORA. It is autobiographical and historical.

White supremacy and white color racism are a worldwide DISEASE. Johann Friedrich Blumenbach was the first to divide humanity based on skin color; Caucasian, Mongolian, Malayan, Ethiopian, and American (Indian). He chose the term Caucasian to represent the Europeans because a skull from the Caucasus Mountains of Russia was, in his opinion, the most beautiful. Thus began the birthof white supremacy.

Chapter 1 deals with the first recorded Genocide of the 20th century. Contrary to popular opinion the Armenian Genocide happened in 1915-1917. The Hereo and Namaqua genocide started in 1904, in what is modern day South West Africa.

Chapter 2 is a discussion about the most ruthless dictator of the 19th and 20th centuries respectively speaking. Was it Hitler, Stalin, Mussolini, or none of the above? The truth is it was the evil King Leopold II. From 1885 to 1908, Leopold and his henchmen were responsible for at least 15 million Black people being torched and killed.

Chapter 3 explores the evil British who sent Arthur Phillip and a group of convicts to Australia where they founded a penal colony, only to colonize and murder the indigenous natives who had been there for65,000 years, namely the Aboriginal people and the Torres Straight Islanders.

Chapter 4 is about 200 years of Chattel Slavery, 100 years of Jim and Jane Crow segregation, 100 years of Discrimination, The infamous Dred Scott Decision, and the infamous Plessy v Ferguson Decision.

Is My Skin The Sin?

Part 2
WHY BLACK PEOPLE CANNOT BE RACIST

Part 3
CURRENT EVENTS

Foreword

We have been saying their names for weeks, months, and decades now. Thanks to the public's instant access to video technology, there are shocking images of many of them that we just cannot unsee.

As our minds try to process the loss of so many promising Black lives at the hands of individuals duly sworn to serve and protect, my friend, Dennis Brown and I find ourselves disaggregating data during every discussion we have on current events. We brainstorm, trying to put our finger directly on exactly what this problem is and how this problem came to be. How do so many promising Black lives that are filled with hope, purpose, dignity; and yes, maybe sometimes sadness, and poverty, become victims of so much racially motivated violence? Brutality that repeatedly leads to their deaths.

Throughout these pages of anecdotal thoughts, autobiographical reflections, and historical data, Dennis Brown analyzes, educates, inspires, and contributes significantly to challenging all of us to find a way forward through the infliction of discrimination.

We are angry and after we express that anger to each other we agree that anger is not and never will be a good medium to resolve the issue. So, we rein those emotions in and try to use every biblical principle we have learned to uplift, encourage, and inspire.

 My name is Dennis James. I am a medical professional and have no formal writing experience. I graduated from TSU School of Pharmacy in 1981 and proceeded to work in retail pharmacy at management and executive levels for the last thirty years. I have also been a preceptor, board member and chairperson, for various HSBC's and professional and government pharmacy organizations in Texas and Virginia. Yet, I too, have experienced the exclusion, alienation, bias, and unfairness all Black professionals deal within Corporate America. Even though this IS a book I could write, Dennis Brown has given me the honor of being a sounding board for his ideas in and about his book. I feel his request is based on the connection we have and the trauma we shared as teens coming of age after the height of the civil rights movement.

Dennis Brown and I met in the early 70's during integration of the Austin Independent School District in Texas. We were young middle school teenage children at the time and consequently we share many of the same unjust and prejudicial experiences. We were bused miles from our homes, arriving at school several hours early and herded into cafeterias and auditoriums for another few hours.Unfortunately, that followed a gauntlet of threats, cursing, spitting, pushing, and insults from white classmates along with their heavily armed adult parents as we departed our buses. The white security staff looked the other way.

During those years in the integrated school systems, we were passed over and intentionally left behind in sports and academics even when we excelled and outperformed our white counterparts. We were wrongfully accused of every infraction imaginable to get us suspended from class or expelled from school, sports, and even the entire school district. Corporal punishment was allowed in schools at the time, and we witnessed white administrators using illegal paddles, paddle students for far too long while illegally administering too many strikes. Black students were always the victims of discipline even when they were innocent and white students were clearly at fault.

Luckily, some of us had strong support systems within our families, communities, and churches that encouraged and grounded us; however, Dennis and I can easily identify approximately 4 out of 10 of our childhood friends who never had a chance to even finish high school. It was not easy for most of us to channel our anger into a desire and action plan to claim our power. All we have ever wanted is our political power, financial power, and social power, like everyone else in America.

Dennis Brown writes in amazingly calm and thoughtful tones as we continue to observe too many occurrences of the same senseless waste of life under the same unjust circumstances.

Over the decades we have clearly witnessed a repetition of seeing our oppressed and marginalized people begin to prosper and to help our brothers and sisters prosper only to have our manpower and resources attacked and drained. Lately though it is empowering and revitalizing to see the real commitment we need from people to get behind us and give support to government policy to confront these issues.
Enjoy this look into the thoughts of an activist minister.

Acts 17:26 NIV
"From one man he made all the nations, that they should inhabit the earth; and he marked out their appointed times in history and the boundaries of their lands"

Dennis James
Virginia Beach, Va.

INTRODUCTION

I remember what it was like growing up as a young Black male in Austin, Texas. My oldest brother and I would watch Art Linkletter's House Party on television. One of our favorite segments on the show was Kids Say the Darndest Things. Mr. Linkletter would ask the children a question and each child gave their answer. One show in particular stands out in my mind. There were 3 young boys and Mr. Linkletter asked each of them what they wanted to be when they grew up. One of the boys, who happened to be Black, answered "he wanted to be a white man" when he grew up. Mr. Linkletter was stunned by the child's answer and asked him why he wanted to be a white man. The young boy replied, "because my mother said a nigger ain't shit". I was 8 years old when I heard this. Fifty plus years later that answer still rings in my mind.

About 25 years ago I started working on my second book, IS MY SKIN THE SIN. However, I had writers block; something was missing so I proceeded to collect data on the history of white supremacy throughout the world. Reflecting upon my own personal experiences with white supremacy I recalled the closing of the only two Black schools in Austin. For the first time in my life, I was bused to a predominantly white school. In order to catch the bus, I had to walk one mile from my home to the bus stop. My extended family was destroyed. This was integration at its worst. The school I was assigned to attend in the 9th grade was Sidney Lanier which was namedafter a Confederate soldier.

I remember learning firsthand that prejudice is a byproduct of white supremacy. While in the 7th grade, at Kealing Jr. High, I was a starting point guard and in the 8th grade I was the 6th man. In the 9th grade at Lanier my life completely changed, I didn't exist. The remaining friends and I from Kealing were all pumped up to begin a new basketball season at Lanier. In the 9th grade, due to the closing of the Black schools, my life completely changed. There was a group of kids from Burnett Junior High who also attended Lanier. They had a terrible basketball team in the 8th grade. The guys from Kealing had embarrassed them the year prior. I know because I was one of the guys. Nevertheless, the coach for the 9th grade team automatically gave the first starting 5 positions to the guys from Burnett. The rest of us had to compete to make the 2nd or 3rd team. This was devastating to me.

Prior to the closing of Kealing my academics were stellar. I worked for the late Senator Barbara Jordan at the State Capital, and I was recognized as one of the best starting point guards in city. My future looked very promising.

When Brown v. Board of Education came down the pike, our Black leaders thought Integration was the way to go. On their part it was the worst decision they could have ever made. No doubt that Segregation was evil and needed to go, however, integration by force was and still is a bad idea.

I remember riots broke out at John H. Reagan High School. One young man lost the sight in his eye, when he was stabbed in the eye with a pencil. A few years earlier white supremacist burned buses in Boston Massachusetts. They were against forced Integration. I was terrified as a young Black male, who weighed about 100 lbs. of going to school with people I did not know. My main friends, for the most part, were sent to other "white plantations". I ended up going to 4 different "white plantations". I finally left school in 1975. It was the year that I was supposed to graduate. Years later I got a GED and subsequently went to HBCU (Huston Tillotson University) and earned a BA degree in Government.

I hope you enjoy my book. I hope it's an eye opener and it gives you some understanding, insight and clarity.

Dennis Brown

Chapter 1

SONG OF SOLOMON
Chapter 1 verses 6&7

I am Black, but comely, O ye daughters of Jerusalem, as the tents of Kedar, as the curtains of Solomon. Look not upon me, because I am black, because the sun hath looked upon me: my mother's children were angry with me; they made me the keeper of the vineyards; but my own vineyard have I not kept.

Several years ago, I was riding down Wilshire Boulevard in Los Angeles California andI saw all these cars with flags flying and helicopters also with flags and banners circling. I wondered to myself about what was going on. As I got closer, I saw that it was people from the Armenian community commemorating the 100-year anniversary of the Armenian genocide. Some of the signs being displayed suggested the Armenian genocide was the first genocide of the 20th Century. I knew however that it was not the first genocide. The Armenian Genocide occurred from 1915 to 1917.

The first genocide of the 20th century was that of Herero (also known as the Ovaherero) and Namaque genocide. It was waged by the German Empire against theOvaherero, the Nama and the San people in Germany's South West Africa (Namibia).It occurred between 1904 and 1908.

In January of 1904, the Herero people rebelled against German colonial rule and killed about 100 German men. In August,1904, the German Lieutenant General Lothar von Trotha, defeated the Herero people at the Battle of Waterberg and drovethem into the desert where most of the people died of dehydration.

In October, of the same year the Nama people rebelled and suffered the same fate. Between 24,000 and 100,000 died in the genocide and numerous others were put in concentration camps where most of them died of disease, sexual and physical abuse as well as exhaustion. Skulls of dead prisoners were sent back to German Laboratories for experimentation to prove the long held racist idea that Black/Africans were inferior to whites. It is reported that 80% of the Herero people and 50% of the Nama people were destroyed.

In 1985 the United Nations declared that what happened to these Blackpeople was the first genocide of the 20th Century.

Is My Skin the Sin? Why are we, as Black people, **Universally Despised?**
What is it about our skin that leads others to want to destroy u

CHAPTER 2

ALL MEN ARE MADE IN THE IMAGE OF GOD AND GOD AS EVERYBODY KNOWS IS NOT A NEGRO

THEREFORE, THE NEGRO CANNOT BE A MANAUTHOR UNKNOWN

I have often asked this question. Who killed more Black people throughout the world?

HITLER
STALIN
MUSSOLINI
NONE OF THE ABOVE

Most people usually say Hitler. Why is that? It is a mystery to me. Then again Hitler has been paraded across the screen and print media for decades. His name is synonymous with murder. He was a murderer who attempted to annihilate the Jewish people. Fortunately, the Jewish people tracked down each one of those Nazis and made them pay for their evil atrocities.

Was it Stalin? Stalin is responsible for mass murders mostly of his own people. In any case, it was not mass murder of Black people. It must have been Mussolini. It was not him even though his fascist ideas are still around. Who then was the greatest mass murderer of Black people? In the period from 1885 to 1908 one of the world's least known atrocities was committed by King Leopold II. He is attributed to being responsible for killing at least 15 million Black people in the Congo Free State (known today as the Democratic Republic of the Congo). This became Leopold II's own personal country.

The country was rich with Rubber and Ivory. A lot of Africans died of disease and famine. Another way many of them died was by having their hands cut off if they did not meet their Rubber collecting quota

CHAPTER 3

HE RODE A PALE HORSE HIS NAME IS DEATH
Revelations 6:8

For over 65,000 years the first people who arrived in Australia were the Aboriginal people and the Torres Strait Islanders. However, around 1770 a British sailor, Captain James Cook, found the fertile coast of Australia. He named it New South Wales and claimed it for the British Empire. The British decided to use the land as a prison colony. They needed the land to house prisoners. During the war of Independence, they lost their American colonies. The first fleet of 11 ships carrying 1500 people arrived in modern day Sydney. During the years 1788 to 1868, 160,000 convicts were brought to Australia.

Around 1790 free immigrants started arriving. Over the years the Australian frontier wars resulted in over 200,000 Aboriginal and Torres Strait people being massacred. The colonist arrived in 1788 and the story is that the wars went on until 1934. To this day the Aboriginal and Torres Strait people are still suffering from "white supremacy". White supremacy is a worldwide disease.
Everywhere white people have gone they have gone to conquer. Is it because all other people are weak? Is it because of their skin color? White supremacy and white color racism have been around for centuries. It has only gotten worse and there looks like there are no signs of it decreasing.

This book is designed to raise awareness on this ever-growing disease in hopes that we might find a cure for it. We found a vaccine for Polio. We found a vaccine for Influenza and currently we have vaccines for COVID 19. Maybe we can find a cure/vaccine for white supremacy.

Chapter 4

Life can be brighter if your skin is Whiter Author Unknown

The cruelest form of human bondage known to mankind in the 16th century was chattel Slavery. There was human slavery in the past, however, chattel slavery was the worst. Black people experienced it for over 200 years.

Imagine being white and you are told you cannot go to a certain hospital because you are white. Imagine being white and told you could drink only from a fountain labeled "for whites "only".

Black people experienced these and other segregated atrocities for more than 100 years. Black people were told because you are three fifths human you do not have the same rights or privileges as white people have a right to.

The Infamous Dred Scott Decision. The Supreme Court issued a decision in March of 1857, which basically said the Black people had no constitutional rights because they were not included in the US CONSTITUTION. This meant even though Dred's owners had taken him from Missouri into Illinois and the Wisconsin Territory (which were areas where slavery was illegal) it did not matter because Dred was still considered a slave and not a free man, as a NIGGER HAD NO RIGHTS.

The infamous Plessy V Ferguson
Plessy V Ferguson was a landmark 1896 US SUPREME COURT decision that upheld the constitutionality of racial segregation under the Separate but Equal doctrine.
Basically, this was the continued practice of white supremacy by the highest court in the land.

Part 2

WHY BLACK PEOPLE CANNOT BE RACISTS

HERE LIES A BLACK MAN WHO FOUGHT THE YELLOW MAN FOR WHAT THE WHITE MAN TOOK FROM THE RED MAN!

AUTHOR UNKNOWN

In 1978 the Supreme Court of the United States of America made another landmark decision in the Bakke. They basically said that affirmative action was constitutional but racial quotas were not. In other words, Black people could not make up for past discrimination with the use of quotas.

The Bakke decision was the beginning of the "white supremacist" movement proclaiming reverse racism and discrimination. White supremacists proclaimed thatBlack people are racists. I have even heard some ignorant Black people call other Black people racists. THIS IS ABSURED. THE ONLY GROUP OF PEOPLE WHO CAN BE
RACIST ARE WHITE PEOPLE. Beginning with Johan F. Blumenbach, a German, who was the first to divide Humanity on the basis of skin color. MR. BLUMENBACH CLASSIFIED FIVE CHIEF RACES OF MANKIND: Caucasian, Ethiopian, Mongolian, Malayan and American Indian. Moreover, he espoused that the Caucasian is the original race.

This is virtually the beginning of white supremacy, with subsequent pseudo madmen masquerading as scientist perpetuating the myth of white supremacy and color racism. However, there are those on the extreme far right who say Black people are racists. Let's get something straight. You must have institutional power to be racist. Black people can hate white people, condemn white people, kill white people, however Black people cannot control the destinies of white people. What do I mean by that? White supremacy has been institutionalized. For the most part many major institutions are controlled by WASP (White Anglo-Saxon Protestants).

In 1923, the famous HOLLYWOODLAND sign was erected to advertise the name of asegregated housing development that later became known as Hollywood. Segregation was a Northern and Southern mandate. Signs were used to indicate where African Americans could legally walk, talk, drink, rest, or eat. Segregated facilities extended from white schools to white graveyards.

When Black folks protested to end segregation the Supreme Court of United States of America upheld the Separate but Equal doctrine which was reaffirmed under the Plessy V Ferguson decision. Separate and unequal was the order of the day. We were never considered equal even with the passage of the 14th amendment to the US Constitution, which was designed specifically for ex slaves.

Harvard, Yale, Princeton, Brown, University of Texas in Austin, Rice, Dartmouth, Stanford, UCLA, and Cornell are controlled by white people. History books prior to the early nineties promote white supremacy, especially in the state of Texas. If Blacks were racists, why were they segregated in the Military? They were forced by the white Federalgovernment to be segregated. Black people do not control municipalities in the United States of America.

"Black Racism" is a myth created by white people to deflect from them being racists. White people control the police, and all other law enforcement entities in the United States. Do not be misled by the fact that some municipalities have a Black police Chief or a Black Mayor or a Black Superintendent of Public Schools. That is token privilege.

1.   **WHEN DID BLACK PEOPLE TELL WHITE PEOPLE THEY COULD NOT VOTE?**

2.   **WHEN DID BLACK PEOPLE TELL WHITE PEOPLE WHAT SCHOOL THEY HAD TOGO TO?**

3.   **WHEN DID BLACK PEOPLE TELL WHITE PEOPLE WHERE THEY COULD LIVE?**

4.   **WHEN DID BLACK PEOPLE TELL WHITE PEOPLE WHO THEY COULD MARRY?**

5.   **WHEN DID BLACK PEOPLE TELL WHITE PEOPLE THAT THEY COULD NOT GET A LOAN TO START THEIR OWN BUSINESS?**

6.   **WHEN DID BLACK PEOPLE TELL WHITE PEOPLE THEY COULD NOT PLAYI NTERCOLLEGIATE SPORTS FOR THE WHITE UNIVERSITIES?**

7.   **WHEN DID BLACK PEOPLE TELL WHITE PEOPLE WHAT TIME THEY HAD BETTER BE IN THEIR HOMES? THIS HAPPENED IN SUNDOWN TOWNS.**

8.   WHEN DID BLACK PEOPLE TELL WHITE PEOPLE WHAT HOTEL THEY
       COILD STAY AT ?

9.   WHEN DID BLACK PEOPLE TELL WHITE PEOPLE THAT THEY HAD TO
       TAKE THEIR HAT OFF WHEN THEY PASSED A WHITE WOMAN THEY
        SAW IN THESTREET?

a.   WHEN DID BLACK PEOPLE KILL WHITE PEOPLE FOR WHISTLING AT A
       BLACK WOMAN? THAT IS WHAT EMMITT TILL WAS KILLED FOR,
       WHISTLING AT A WHITE WOMAN.

WHITE PEOPLE ARE THE ONLY GROUP OF PEOPLE THAT CAN BE RACIST. WHITE
PEOPLE HAVE INSTITUTIONALIZE "WHITE SUPREMACY AND WHITE SUPREMACY
PERMEATES EVERY AREA OF LIFE!

Part 3
Current Events

Luke 10:18
Jesus says, I saw Satan fall like lighting from heaven.

BLACK LIVES MATTER

The Black Lives Matter movement made a critical error when they chose the phrase "Defund the Police". A better phrase would have gotten their point across without much debate. However, the current Mayor of Los Angeles agreed to defund the police. That meant to take some of the department's money and reallocate it to other areas that would reduce the need for violent responses. For example, mental health issues that police find themselves involved with. Those on the right and those in the middle mistook the phrase to mean abolish the police all together. That is the problem the current officials in Minnesota find themselves in.

Gangsters with Guns and the Unions and the System that condones them.

Since 2005 there have been 3 police officers who have been convicted of murder. These are the exceptions, not the rule. What is it that creates this culture ofviolence by those who are sworn to uphold and protect?

I personally was involved in a protest with the Black Citizens Task Force and the Brown Berets. Two plain clothes officers were eating barbecue at an establishment on east 11th street in Austin, Texas. The two officers, Donavan and Hooker, attempted to arrest **Gil Couch** for public drunkenness after he lunged at them repeatedly in the restaurant where they were eating lunch. According to witnesses one of the officers called for a uniform officer to come and arrest him. Upon trying to arrest Gil Couch a struggle broke out and one officer held him in a choke hold for at least 3 to 4 minutes. After that Couch was pronounced dead at the scene. His autopsy revealed a fractured larynx, and the cause of death was listed as asphyxiation.

The police later admitted that they had never identified themselves to Couch as police officers. When I got a call from the Black Citizens Task Force asking me if I would get involve. I did. We organized daily protests in front of the Police department. This went on for 6 weeks. We made a makeshift casket out of cardboard, and I did the eulogy on the steps of the Austin Police Department. Our protest led to the resignation of the Chief of Police, Frank Dyson. We also created a citizen review board that reviewed policy and procedures of police cadets.

The Couch incident also led to the enactment of a policy that all deaths caused by APD be brought before a grand jury. No disciplinary action was taken. The grand jury declined to indict.

Both officers later quit the force. Hooker cited as his reason for resignation loss of public support for officers and increasing complication of the job. What is it about some police officers when they draw their guns it usually leads to murder of Black people?

What about **George Floyd** who was killed by officer Derek Chauvin after officer Chauvin kneeled on Mr. Floyd's neck for 9 minutes and 29 seconds?

What is it about the police officer who shot and killed **Daunte Wright** claiming she mistook her Glock for a Taser?

What caused police to shoot in the dark and kill **Breonna Taylor**?

What about **Atatiana Jefferson** who was at home with her front door open when police shot and killed her?

What about **Stephon Clark** who was standing in his grandmother's back yardwhen officers arrived? He was shot and killed because the officers thought the mobile phone, he was holding was a gun.

What about **Bothan Jean** who was seated on his sofa at home eating ice cream when he was shot by an officer who thought she was entering her apartment.

What about **Philando Castile** who was pulled over during a traffic stop. He informed the officer who pulled him over that he had a gun as well as the permit to carry a concealed weapon. Nevertheless, the officer shot and killed him.

What about **Freddie Gray** who was killed in a van while in police custody.

What about **Eric Garner** who was allegedly selling loose cigarettes? Officer Daniel Pantaleo held Eric Garner in a choke hold despite Garner saying "I can't breathe 11 times.

What about **Tamir Rice** who was playing with a toy gun in the park? Within 2 seconds he was murdered.

IS MY SKIN THE SIN? ARE WE UNIVERSALLY DESPISED?

The total number of Black People Killed by Police From 2017 to April 2021, is 938

Is Police Reform Working

The short answer is NO! More police training is not the answer. Kim Potter had been with the Minnesota Police Department for 26 years. She was also training a new officer the day she murdered Duante Wright. So obviously more training is not the solution.

When I studied Cadet training of the Austin Police Department, the training focused on defending the officer. The conversation about training and use of tasers missed the point and reinforces the idea that some officers are simply "bad apples". The problem primarily is the culture of policing. Crime is narrowly defined as activity which happens in poorer communities. The function of the police then is to control poor populations of color with either the threat or use of violence. No amount of training will change that mentality. What then are some solutions?

> i. Get rid of Qualified Immunity. Government officials need to be held liable when they violate constitutional rights. If I am a government employee, in this case a police officer, and I work for the city, why should the city pay for my sins of murder? The individual who committed the act should. If a doctor or attorney must have malpracticeinsurance, so should police officers.
>
> ii. Get police off traffic stops. Too many Black lives have been lost to trafficstops. We need a traffic division without guns.
>
> iii. Police officers should have degrees and minor in one of the Social Sciences.
>
> iv. Prospective police officers should be required to take an independent psychological exam by an outside independent consulting firm that is not under contract with the City.
>
> v. A citizen review board with complete transparency and subpoena power.

There have been over 150 unarmed Black Men and Black Women killed by the police since 2000.

Are we as Black people UNIVERSALLY DESPISED? IS MY SKIN THE SIN?

D W. Brown is a native of Austin, Texas. He attended Huston Tillotson College where he earned a B.A. degree in Political Science. Prior to him moving to Los Angeles, Mr. Brown worked for the late Texas State Senators Barbara Jordan and Charles Wilson. Hollywood in fact made a movie about the late Senator Wilson titled Charlie Wilson's War. Additionally, Mr. Brown served as a member of Austin Interfaith, founded by the late Saul Alinksy's Organization: Industrial Area Foundation of New York, New York. Austin Interfaith was a political organization dedicated to helping those who could not help themselves. Mr. Brown served as a Board member of the Austin Branch of Operation PUSH and he was also a staff writer for the Villager Newspaper.

His work with the youth led him to develop and implement a "Rites of Passage" program for boys and girls in both Austin and Houston. This is the second work to Mr. Brown's credit with his first work titled "What The Resurrection of Jesus Should Mean to Black People." He is also the CEO of Schroder Enterprises and Consumer Consultants.

Additional copies of this booklet may be purchased at Barnes and Nobel and Amazon

CPSIA information can be obtained
at www.ICGtesting.com
Printed in the USA
BVHW012313270322
632258BV00010B/148/J